VIKING RAIDERS

Anne Civardi and James Graham-Campbell
Illustrated by Stephen Cartwright

Edited by Abigail Wheatley
Designed by Sarah Cronin and John Jamieson

CONTENTS

D0580710

GOING BACK IN TIME

Have you ever wondered what it would be like to travel back in time and visit people from the past? It's easy when you have a magic helmet. All you have to do is put it on, press the right buttons, and off you go.

You may have heard about the ferocious Vikings who lived in northern Europe many years ago. In just a few seconds you can travel back over 1,000 years, to come face-to-face with some Vikings from the year 890.

You will be able to find out what these people were like, and discover how they lived and what they did. When you want to come home, just press the Emergency Getaway Button on your helmet.

1 THE TIME HELMET

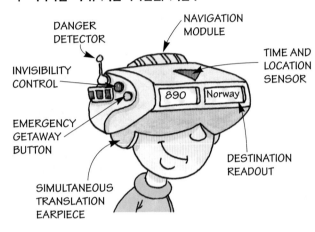

DANGER DETECTOR

NAVIGATION MODULE

INVISIBILITY CONTROL

TIME AND LOCATION SENSOR

EMERGENCY GETAWAY BUTTON

890   Norway

DESTINATION READOUT

SIMULTANEOUS TRANSLATION EARPIECE

2 PICK A DESTINATION

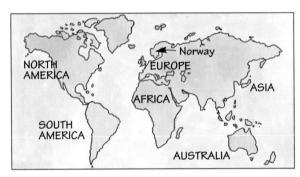

NORTH AMERICA   EUROPE   Norway   ASIA   AFRICA   SOUTH AMERICA   AUSTRALIA

As you can see, the time helmet has lots of useful gadgets. Set the Destination Readout to 'Norway, 890', and enable the Navigation Module. You're off! As you travel back in time, things begin to change...

3 GO!

1940

This is northwest Europe in 1940. There is no television because they are still quite rare. You can see that both the plane and the radio look different from ones today.

1900

Now you have gone back another 40 years things are rather different. Not everyone has electricity, so there are gas lamps and a fire. All the women wear skirts.

1600

Now you have jumped back three centuries. Candles give some light, but they are very expensive. Even glass is a luxury - notice the small window and tiny panes.

1200

You have come a long way now. There is no glass in the windows, and no chimney for the fire: it's rather dark, smoky and cold. Next stop, Viking Norway!

THE PEOPLE YOU WILL MEET

The Vikings you will meet in this book live in Norway. Other Vikings live in Sweden and Denmark too. Together, these places make up Scandinavia.

Life is hard for Vikings, because the winters are long and cold. It is difficult to grow food, and there isn't enough good farm land to go around.

Most Viking men are fierce warriors. During the summer, they sail across the sea to raid other countries. They trade the loot for food and other goods.

ASTRID

Astrid is married to Knut. When she was younger, she went with him on his travels. Now, while he is away raiding, she takes care of the farm and the family. Astrid is a great cook. She also brews beer, and spins and weaves.

KNUT

Erik Knutsson is 22. He is the eldest son of the family. One day the farm will be his, so now he is learning how to run it. But he's good with his sword, too.

ERIK

Earl Knut is the most important chieftain in his part of Norway. He owns a lot of farm land. Knut is very rich - he often goes raiding in Britain and Ireland to steal treasure and capture slaves. He is a fierce warrior, but he is kind to his family, working hard to give them a comfortable life.

SVEN

Björn is the youngest son, at 19. Knut has given him a ship so he can take his family to settle in Iceland. There's not enough land for him to farm in Norway.

BJÖRN

Sven, the second son, is 21 years old. He is wild and brave, and enjoys going on raids with his father. He wants to be wealthy one day too. He is also a trader and sells soapstone bowls, stolen treasure and slaves at the big Viking trading towns.

COUSIN OLAF

FREYDA

Freyda Knutsdaughter is 16 years old. She is learning to cook, brew, spin and weave just like her mother. Freyda also helps look after her younger sisters, Helga and Thora. They learn useful skills at home on the farm. There are no schools - even Knut can't read or write.

Olaf is Knut's cousin. He is also an important chietain, and owns a big farm and his own warship for raiding. People call him Olaf Strongarm, because he is famous for his great strength at fighting.

Knut has lots of help on his farm. His family and the freemen who live nearby all work together to get things done. Knut also takes his sons and some freemen on his raids.

Freemen don't have their own land, but they have houses on Knut's. In return, they help with all the jobs on the farm, and some go raiding with Knut.

MAGNUS

Magnus is the most important freeman on Knut's farm. He is a blacksmith, and makes weapons, and cooking and farming tools.

OLEG

Oleg is learning to be a blacksmith and he helps Magnus in the forge. But his bad temper often gets him into trouble.

Slaves do the nastiest, dirtiest work on the farm. Knut has twelve slaves, but when he goes raiding he will capture some more.

KNUT'S FARM

You have jumped back in time to the year 890 AD. Your time travel helmet has brought you to Earl Knut's farm on the shores of southern Norway. The long, cold winter is over and everyone is busy working on the land. There is lots to do now that the snow has melted.

Knut lives here with his wife Astrid, their six children and all their grandchildren. They live in the main house, which is called the longhouse.

Knut has many slaves and freemen to help him on the farm. All the slaves live together in a small stone hut close to the main house. The freemen have come from their own houses on the Earl's land. Some of their wives and children help Astrid with the housework and cooking in Knut's longhouse.

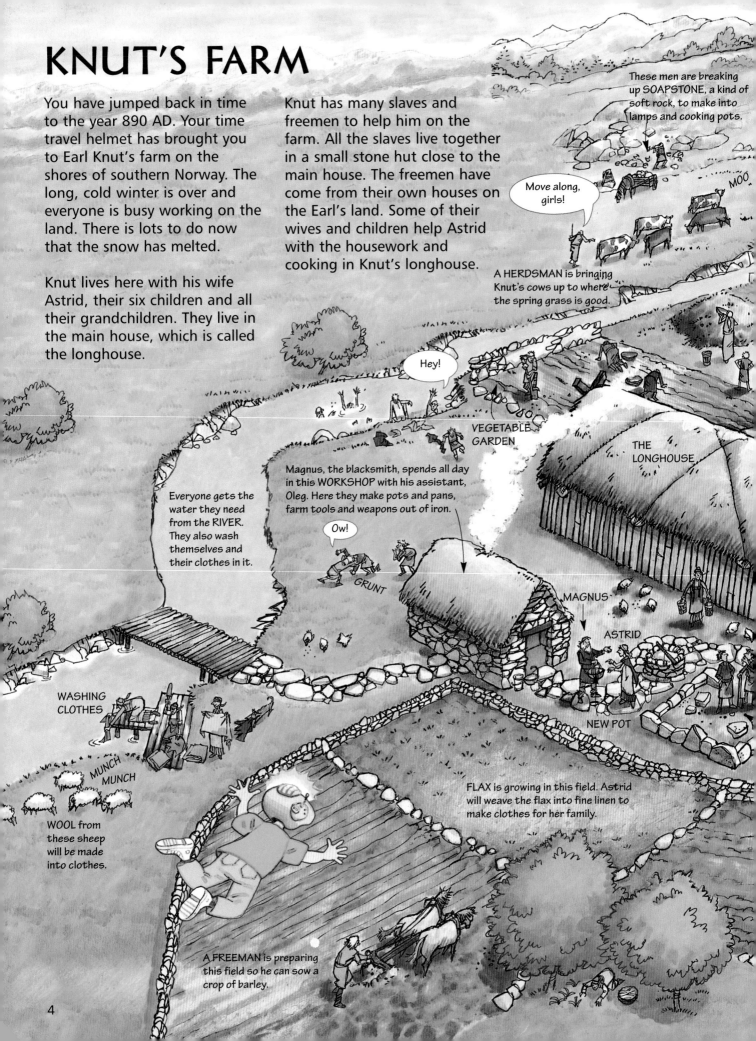

These men are breaking up SOAPSTONE, a kind of soft rock, to make into lamps and cooking pots.

Move along, girls!

MOO

A HERDSMAN is bringing Knut's cows up to where the spring grass is good.

Hey!

VEGETABLE GARDEN

THE LONGHOUSE

Everyone gets the water they need from the RIVER. They also wash themselves and their clothes in it.

Magnus, the blacksmith, spends all day in this WORKSHOP with his assistant, Oleg. Here they make pots and pans, farm tools and weapons out of iron.

Ow!

GRUNT

MAGNUS

ASTRID

NEW POT

WASHING CLOTHES

MUNCH MUNCH

WOOL from these sheep will be made into clothes.

FLAX is growing in this field. Astrid will weave the flax into fine linen to make clothes for her family.

A FREEMAN is preparing this field so he can sow a crop of barley.

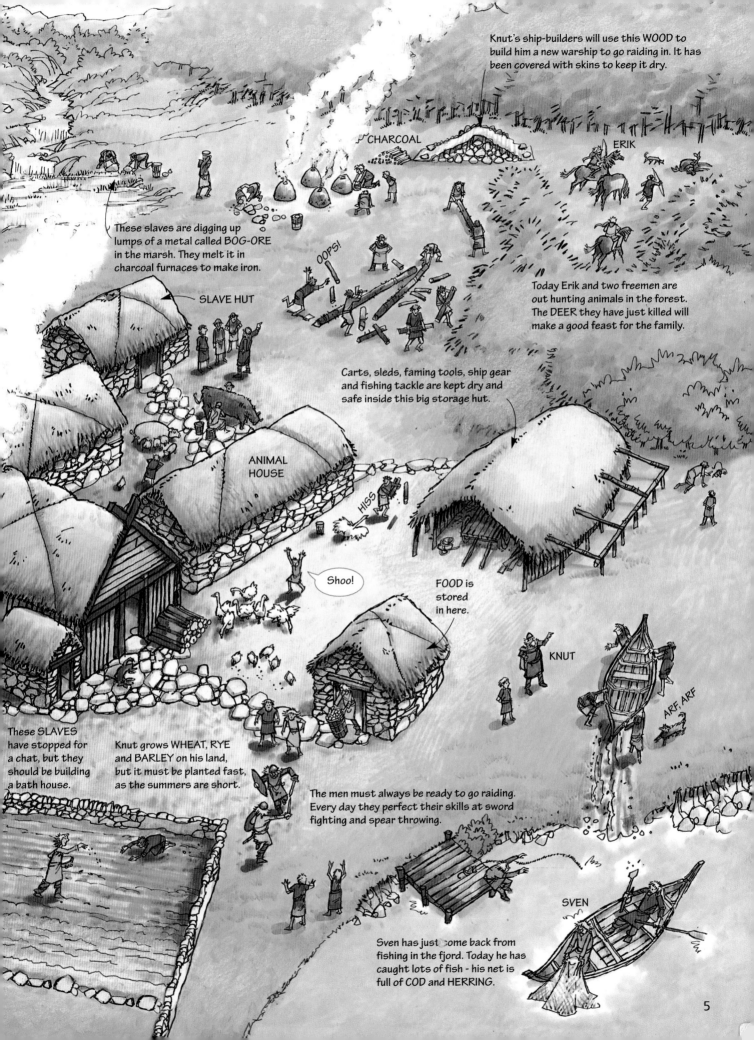

INSIDE KNUT'S LONGHOUSE

Earl Knut and his family live together in the longhouse. The one room is always dark, smoky and rather smelly, as the windows are very small. A hole in the roof lets out the smoke from the big fire.

While he waits for his morning meal, the Earl is carving arrows. Astrid is weaving the last length of wool for the sail of Knut's new ship. Erik is already out working hard on the farm.

At one end of the longhouse, the women are busy preparing and cooking the food. Today, the family will eat hot barley and oat porridge, fresh bread rolls and new butter, cheese and milk.

Everyone else sleeps on the raised platforms at the side of the house. There is very little furniture. They keep all their things in big wooden chests.

Knut and Astrid have a proper BED.

KNUT

BJÖRN

YAWN!

OIL LAMP

SLAVE

MILK

EEEK

FLOUR

MAKING BREAD

HOLE TO PUT IN THE GRAIN

FLOUR

QUERN

This woman is grinding barley in a big stone quern. She turns the handle until it is ground into flour.

KNEADING TROUGH

Next she mixes the flour with water and kneads it together in a big wooden trough to make dough for bread.

METAL PAN

When the dough is mixed, she shapes it into small loaves and bakes them over the hot ashes of the fire.

MAKING WOOL INTO THREAD

SHEARS

METAL COMB

SPINDLE

This stick is known as a DISTAFF.

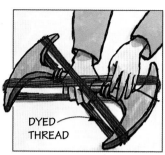

DYED THREAD

In the early summer, Sven shears the sheep with metal shears. Freyda washes the wool.

Then Freyda combs it with long metal combs to get rid of any knots and twigs.

Astrid ties some wool to a stick and uses a spindle to pull out long pieces of twisted thread.

She wraps the thread around a yarn-winder. Sometimes it is dyed with vegetable juices.

Eric's wife is beating flax to break it into short threads. Then she will spin it into a long thread to be woven into cloth.

FLAX

ASTRID WEAVING CLOTH

HOT PORRIDGE

Freyda is ironing the clothes. The IRON is a heated lump of glass, and the BOARD is made of whalebone.

BAKING BREAD

SOAPSTONE LOOM WEIGHTS

BUTTER AND CHEESE

After a hard day's work, everyone will be very hungry. Soon the women will start cooking the evening meal of meat, wild vegetables and fruit.

Astrid spends hours each day at her LOOM. She makes cloth for sails, clothes and blankets. Girls learn to spin and weave at a young age.

BUILDING A WARSHIP

Today, Earl Knut has come to watch his freemen building a new warship. They have been hard at work for many weeks, but it is nearly finished.

Long before work began, trees of the right shape were carefully chosen, felled, and then left to dry out. Now the men are fixing the last planks.

The warship must be strong enough to cross the rough open sea to Ireland, with enough room for 40 men to live on board during the trip.

OLD WARSHIP

BOATHOUSE

Carpenters use tools called adzes to shape a long, thick MAST.

THWACK!

CARVED STERN POST

MAKING OARS

Oh dear!

The ship is about 24m (80ft) long, and 5m (16ft) wide.

Look out!

The ship-builders have made holes for OARS along the sides. When the ship is sailing, little wooden discs cover the holes to keep out the water.

FUMBLE

STEERING OAR

HOW A SHIP IS BUILT

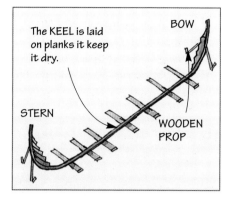

The KEEL is laid on planks it keep it dry.

BOW

STERN

WOODEN PROP

The trunk of tall oak tree is shaped to form the bottom of the boat, called the keel. A curved piece of wood is joined to the front to make the bow. Another is joined to the back to make the stern.

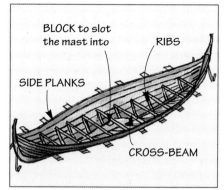

BLOCK to slot the mast into

RIBS

SIDE PLANKS

CROSS-BEAM

Carpenters cut long, light planks from pine trees, and attach them with rivets to the keel, the bow and the stern. Supports called ribs and cross-beams are fitted. A huge block is added to hold the mast.

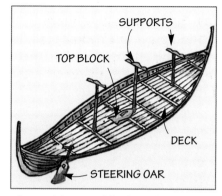

SUPPORTS

TOP BLOCK

DECK

STEERING OAR

They add a top block to help keep the mast upright. They make the oar holes, join on the steering oar, and lay the deck. Last, they add supports for storing the mast and sail when they are not in use.

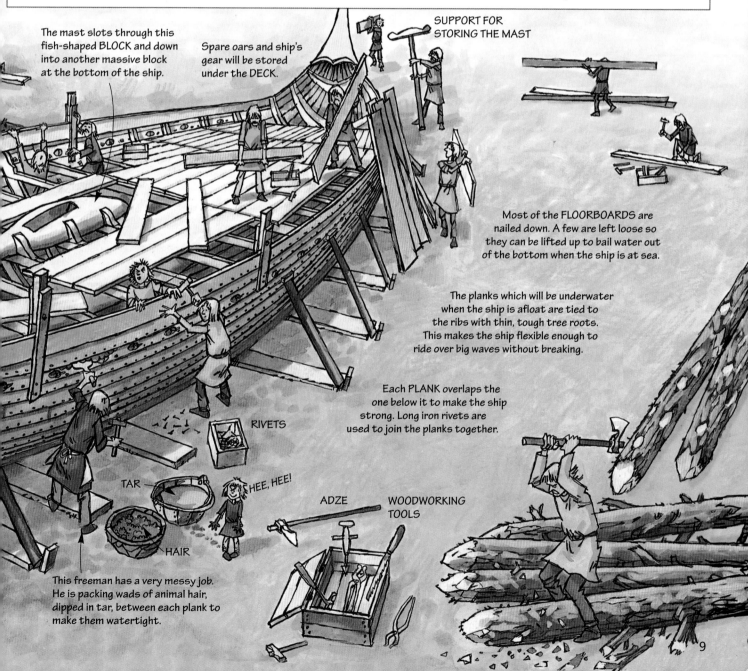

The mast slots through this fish-shaped BLOCK and down into another massive block at the bottom of the ship.

Spare oars and ship's gear will be stored under the DECK.

SUPPORT FOR STORING THE MAST

Most of the FLOORBOARDS are nailed down. A few are left loose so they can be lifted up to bail water out of the bottom when the ship is at sea.

The planks which will be underwater when the ship is afloat are tied to the ribs with thin, tough tree roots. This makes the ship flexible enough to ride over big waves without breaking.

Each PLANK overlaps the one below it to make the ship strong. Long iron rivets are used to join the planks together.

RIVETS

TAR

HEE, HEE!

HAIR

ADZE

WOODWORKING TOOLS

This freeman has a very messy job. He is packing wads of animal hair, dipped in tar, between each plank to make them watertight.

THE RAIDERS GET READY

At last Earl Knut's new ship is finished. Now he can go raiding. His three sons, Erik, Sven and Björn, and his most trusted freemen will go with him. Olaf, Knut's cousin, and two other chieftains have brought their warships too.

They and their warriors will join the raiders. Everyone hurries to finish the final preparations. While the warriors are away, Astrid and the others will have plenty of work to do, looking after the farm.

Magnus the blacksmith is making and mending weapons for the raiders. His assistant, Oleg, keeps the charcoal fire hot with bellows.

When the iron is red hot, Magnus takes it off the fire with his tongs and beats it into shape on the anvil. This weapon is a present for Cousin Olaf.

Magnus decorates special axes, spears and swords with gold and silver for chiefs. He can spend up to a month working on his best ones.

The Vikings are very proud of being good fighters and owning fine weapons. Even young boys learn how to fight. Today is the last time for Knut and his men to train before they go off on the raids.

They all have swords, spears, axes and shields. Some also have bows and arrows. A few warriors have throwing spears to hurl at the enemy, and others have spears specially made for thrusting.

A Viking raider's most precious possession is his sword. It is a sharp and deadly weapon. Only important men, such as Knut and Olaf, wear shirts made of chain mail and metal helmets in battle.

LOADING UP THE SHIP

Everyone helps to load up the new warship. The raiders pack all the things they will need to use on the long voyage.

Very little food is carried on board - just a few barrels of water and milk, some flour and some dried fish and meat. Knut and his men will steal the food they need as they raid.

Between the raids, the warriors will camp on shore, keeping close to their ships for a quick get-away.

The raiders keep their things inside SEA CHESTS, but they also use them as seats when they are rowing the ship.

FURS FOR WARM BEDDING

FREYDA

Ow!

MILK

GRRRR

Let go!

These bags are full of dried strips of FISH and MEAT.

Knut's BED is packed, but everyone else will have to sleep on the ground.

COOKING THINGS

COLLAPSIBLE STAND FOR CAULDRON

There's no cooking on the ship, as it might catch fire, but the raiders take their cooking things so they can have a hot meal when they are on land.

WOODWORKING TOOLS

BJÖRN

ASTRID

That way!

ERIK

OIL LAMP

KNUT

SVEN

COUSIN OLAF

MAGNUS GIVES OLAF HIS PRESENT

11

SETTING OFF

At dawn the next day, the chieftains and their warriors begin the long, hard voyage to Ireland. It's a good day for sailing, with a clear sky and a strong wind behind them.

Knut is excited about spending the summer raiding. But Astrid and the other women are sad to see the men go. Some may not return. They may be killed in battle or drown at sea.

The raiders will spend several days living and sleeping on their ships out of sight of land. It is very cramped on board and they will have an uncomfortable journey.

SEA CHESTS USED AS SEATS

LOOKOUT

Rocks to starboard!

COUSIN OLAF

In shallow water the STEERING OAR must be lifted clear of the bottom.

Cousin Olaf is HELMSMAN on his ship. As the men row, he guides it down the fjord, past dangerous rocks near the shore, using the steering oar.

Go safely!

SVEN

FREYDA

Knut and Astrid say goodbye.

Bye!

LIFE ON BOARD

Ship life is very boring when the weather is calm and the wind is blowing in the right direction. There's nothing much to do except eat, sleep and fish. At night the men sleep on deck in sleeping bags made of skin. They take turns to keep watch for land.

This ship is now leaving the FJORD and heading for the open sea. Its big sail is lashed to a long pole called the yard. The crew turns the sail to catch the wind, using ropes attached to the corners of the yard.

YARD

If possible, the Vikings sail along coasts. But when they sail out of sight of land, they use the SUN and the STARS to navigate, and watch for coastal birds to show them that land is near. They also have a kind of SUNDIAL which they use to tell them the direction to sail in.

Some crew members keep their oars in the water to steady the ship.

Good luck!

It's tricky raising the MAST - it's very heavy and might unbalance the ship.

SPLASH

SEALS

OARS

SHOVE

As the ship moves slowly over the LOGS, the men pick up those at the back and lay them in front of the ship.

ERIK

HEAVE

Erik is in charge of his father's new WARSHIP. Slaves help him and the crew to push it into the water.

13

RAID!

The raiders had a good voyage and they are now in Ireland. They have found a rich monastery to rob of its treasures. The younger warriors hope to win fame by fighting bravely, seizing riches and prisoners to take home.

When they saw the Viking warships, the terrified people from nearby farms fled to the walled monastery for safety. But the monks are more used to praying than fighting. They sent a runner off to fetch help.

The raiders have set fire to the buildings to force the people out. They must finish their attack quickly and get away before the news of their arrival spreads.

NOBLEMAN'S FORT

Some of the Vikings ride off on stolen horses to raid a nearby nobleman's house.

This herdsman is trying to drive his SHEEP away, to save them from the raiders.

Knut has snatched the treasure from the church. The gold ALTAR CROSS and GOSPEL BOOK will fetch a good price in Norway. He will give the CASKET to Astrid.

SCHOOLHOUSE FOR YOUNG MONKS

THE CHURCH

BJÖRN

SQUAWK

KNUT

ERIK

SVEN

Erik and Sven have found a hoard of treasure the monks tried to hide. When they next go trading they will exchange the SILVER PLATES and COINS for valuable goods.

A FEAST

At the end of the summer, Knut and his warriors sailed back to Norway. Their ship was loaded with goods and prisoners from lots of successful raids.

Astrid has made a huge feast to celebrate their return. For days the women have worked hard cooking mountains of food. As it is such a special occasion, cows and sheep have been killed, and deer and boars brought in from the forest. Astrid has cooked the meat in lots of different ways.

Knut invited the other chieftains to the feast. But Cousin Olaf has gone home. He was wounded badly in the raid and is very ill.

Even so, everyone wears their best clothes and jewels for the feast. The longhouse rings with laughter and song, as raiders tell stories of their bravery and cunning against the enemy, the terrible storms at sea, and the strange lands and people they have seen.

DRINKING HORN

Your health!

Skål!

GLUG

This cook is braising WILD BOAR steaks.

HOME BREWED BEER

ROAST SHEEP

SLICES OF BEEF

Everyone gets very messy eating with their fingers, but some guests have KNIVES or wooden SPOONS. They drink from carved cow HORNS, GLASSES or wooden CUPS.

GAME BOARD

KNUT'S GIFTS TO ASTRID

SILVER NECKLACE

GLASS BEADS

GOLD BRACELETS

GOLD RINGS

SHAWL BROOCHES

STOLEN NECKLACE

BRONZE BROOCHES

Since the raiders returned Magnus, the blacksmith, has been very busy. He melts down the gold coins and silver bowls over the hot charcoals of his fire.

Then he works the precious metals into brooches, necklaces and bracelets for Astrid. Knut has also stolen some jewels on his raids, and given them to Astrid to wear.

ASTRID'S CASKET

RUNES

This is Astrid's new jewel box, stolen from the monastery. The words *Astridr a kistu thasa* (Astrid owns this casket) have been carved on it, in Viking letters known as runes.

COOKING MEAT

SPIT ROASTED

First a kitchen slave removes the animal's head, feet and insides. Then he puts it on a long iron rod and roasts it, turning it over the fire.

BAKED

Sometimes meat is baked in a big hole in the ground. Hot stones are packed around the meat and covered with earth until the meat is cooked.

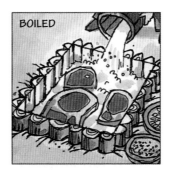

BOILED

To boil meat, the cook fills a wood-lined pit with water and puts in chunks of meat. Herbs like mustard seeds, cumin and garlic are added.

HOT STONES

Then the cook drops in hot stones from the fire, to heat up the water and cook the meat. Boiling meat like this takes quite a long time.

COUSIN OLAF DIES

Cousin Olaf is lying in bed. The arrow wound he got on the raid is very bad. At his bedside, Knut and Astrid pray to the Viking gods to save his life.

They believe their gods are magnificent heroes, who can perform great feats of strength and magic and who are fearless warriors.

Olaf's relatives beg Thor, god of thunder, and Odin, chief of the gods, to answer their prayers. Without their help, Olaf Strongarm will die.

Olaf has a lucky charm hanging around his neck to keep evil spirits away. It is shaped like Thor's hammer.

Thor, son of Odin, you killed the great giant Hrungnir...

STATUE

Olaf's relatives pray to THOR and give his statue offerings of wine and food. Thor rules the thunder, winds and lightning. He carries a huge hammer, named MJOLLNIR, which means lightning. Thor rides across the sky in a chariot drawn by goats.

GUTHRUN, OLAF'S WIFE

ASTRID

KNUT

Yuk!

HOT WATER

A DOCTOR changes the bandages on Olaf's wounded arm. He knows how to mend broken bones and clean sword cuts. As he works, he chants magic spells.

OLAF'S HUNTING DOG

Olaf's daughter looks after the HERBAL DRINK the doctor has made to treat her father.

BURIAL PREPARATIONS

Prayers and medicine did not save Olaf's life. Guthrun is grief-stricken as she prepares his body for burial. Olaf will be buried in his best clothes and his finest jewels.

SNIFF

Olaf's body is carried to the family cemetery in a horse-drawn wagon. His father - also a great chieftain - and his mother were buried there when they died.

Two of Olaf's finest horses and his faithful hunting dog are led away to be killed. The Viking people believe they will live again with Olaf in his after-life.

THE BURIAL

Olaf was a famous and wealthy man, so he is buried with his warship. A special chamber has been built on the deck of the ship for his body to lie in.

Vikings believe that people have another life after they die. Olaf's most treasured possessions have been buried with him, so he can use them in this life-after-death.

Olaf will probably live in Valhalla, the Viking heaven, where warriors feast in Odin's great hall.

SOIL TO FILL IN THE GRAVE

OLAF'S MOTHER IS BURIED HERE.

OLAF'S FATHER IS BURIED HERE.

Stop that!

SOB!

HOW OTHER VIKINGS WERE BURIED

Poor people are usually buried in a big hole with a few of their belongings. This woman has been buried with two spindles, a comb and a barrel of milk.

Sometimes dead warriors are burned on a pile of wood, called a pyre. Their swords and spears are broken, their shields slashed and thrown onto the pyre with them.

This grave for a rich farmer is tidily lined with wood. The slave curled up at the side was killed to be buried with her master. Very few slaves die like this.

BJÖRN SAILS TO ICELAND

It is springtime again, and Bjorn is setting off with his family to go and live in Iceland. Some freemen and slaves are going too, to help build a house and work on the land.

In Norway, most of the good land is already being farmed. There isn't much left for young farmers and their families. So many people have left to settle and farm in other countries.

It will take Björn several weeks to reach Iceland. He will sail in the new ship his father has given him. It has a big hold in the deck to carry all the cargo Björn is taking.

1 GETTING READY TO LEAVE

As well as household things and clothes, Björn is loading some animals for breeding in Iceland. He is also taking animal food, farming tools, and barley seeds to plant.

2 VISITING THE SHETLANDS

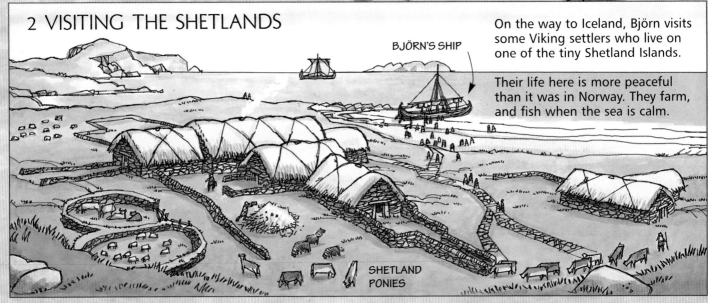

On the way to Iceland, Björn visits some Viking settlers who live on one of the tiny Shetland Islands.

Their life here is more peaceful than it was in Norway. They farm, and fish when the sea is calm.

3 SHIPWRECKED ON THE FAROES

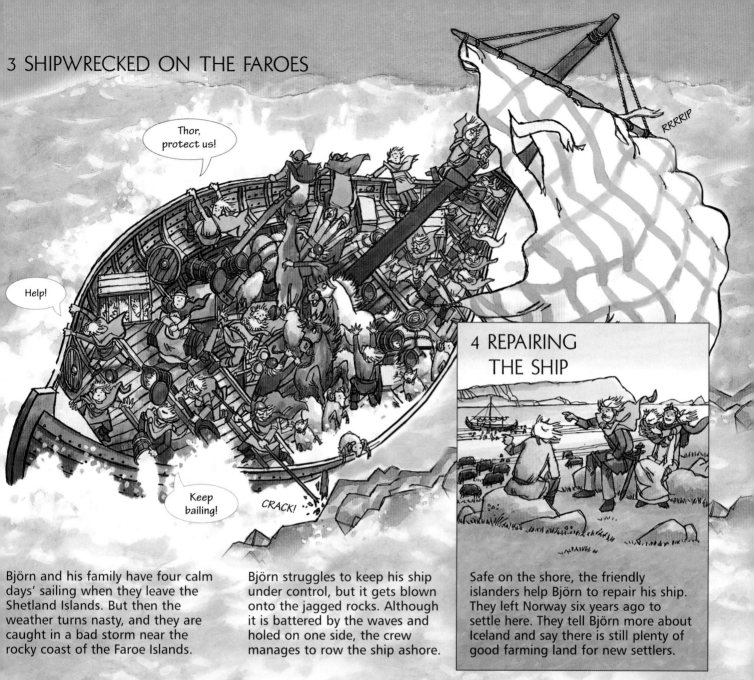

Björn and his family have four calm days' sailing when they leave the Shetland Islands. But then the weather turns nasty, and they are caught in a bad storm near the rocky coast of the Faroe Islands.

Björn struggles to keep his ship under control, but it gets blown onto the jagged rocks. Although it is battered by the waves and holed on one side, the crew manages to row the ship ashore.

4 REPAIRING THE SHIP

Safe on the shore, the friendly islanders help Björn to repair his ship. They left Norway six years ago to settle here. They tell Björn more about Iceland and say there is still plenty of good farming land for new settlers.

5 ARRIVING IN ICELAND

When the ship is ready, Björn sets off once again. After many days at sea, he sees Iceland on the horizon. It is a strange island, with plumes of smoke and steam from volcanoes, and treeless, snow-topped mountains.

As he sails around the south coast, Björn finds that all the flat land there has already been taken. But further west, he discovers some unclaimed land that looks good for farming.

SVEN GOES TRADING

After another summer of raiding, Sven takes his wife down the coast to the big trading town of Hedeby. It's an exciting place, full of Viking merchants exchanging goods.

With his share of the loot - six young, healthy slaves and a bag of silver - Sven hopes to buy silk cloth and other costly things that come from foreign countries. Knut has also given him some soapstone bowls from the farm to sell.

Some Arab merchants have come overland all the way from Asia to sell silk and buy slaves to take back home. Merchants come from far and wide with different goods.

In many parts of the town, craftsmen are hard at work making combs, leather shoes and wool cloth to trade. Clay pots, amber beads, farm tools, ropes and weapons are also on sale. It's a good place for catching up on news, too!

SHIPS OF VISITING MERCHANTS

SVEN'S CAMP

TRADING SHIPS

FISH

WATCHING FOR INVADERS

This wooden fence keeps out enemies and protects the ships.

Most of the houses in Hedeby are made of WATTLE and DAUB (sticks woven together and packed with mud). Some are made from split TREE-TRUNKS.

SVEN BUYS SILK AND WINE

I wonder how much I'm worth...

SVEN

ARM BANDS

ARAB TRADER SELLING SILK

Sven will sell these soapstone bowls later.

WINE

BERGDIS

Sven is buying wine and drinking glasses. They are for the winter festival which will be held at Knut's farm. In exchange he gives three slaves and some silver arm bands.

The trader weighs the silver to find out how much it is worth. The arm bands are worth the same as equal weights of coins. Bergdis, Sven's wife, also wants to buy some silk.

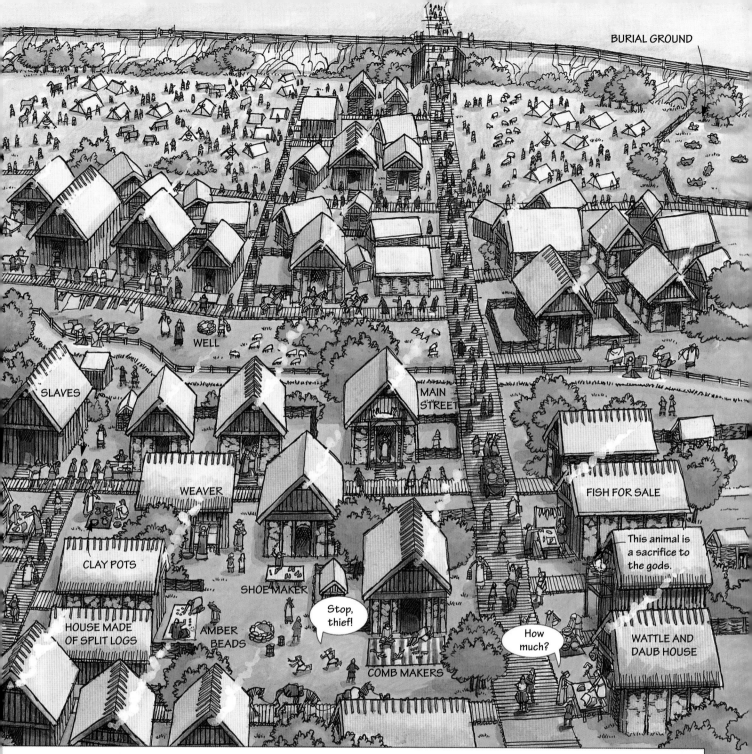

BURIAL GROUND

WELL

SLAVES

MAIN STREET

BAA

WEAVER

FISH FOR SALE

CLAY POTS

SHOE MAKER

This animal is a sacrifice to the gods.

HOUSE MADE OF SPLIT LOGS

AMBER BEADS

Stop, thief!

How much?

COMB MAKERS

WATTLE AND DAUB HOUSE

MAKING COMBS

ANTLER

This craftsman is making combs out of deer antlers. He cuts the points off the antler and shaves down the rough outside.

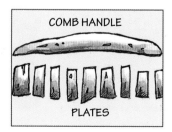

COMB HANDLE

PLATES

Then he carves a smooth, flat strip to make the handle of the comb, and cuts small plates to be made into the teeth.

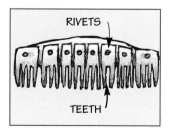

RIVETS

TEETH

He rivets the plates to the handle, and then cuts them into fine teeth. Finally, he decorates the comb with carvings.

COMB CASES

SPOONS

Craftsmen also make comb cases, spoons and knife handles out of bone. They sell them to traders who come to town.

BJÖRN SETTLES IN ICELAND

Björn and his family have been in Iceland for almost three months. At first they camped while the freemen and slaves built a farmhouse. Now they have all moved in to it.

When the summer ends, things get very busy in Iceland. Some settlers who live nearby have come to help Björn get things ready before the winter begins. They cut the grass to make into hay. Björn's animals will need lots of food if they are to survive the long, cold winter.

All summer, the sheep, cows and goats were grazing in the meadows. Now they are driven down to the farm for shelter. Any weak ones are killed. The family will eat their meat during the winter, and save the hay for the other animals.

Björn's wife, Edda, is worried that the family may not have enough food to last the winter. She dries fish on racks in the wind, and packs salted and pickled meat into barrels.

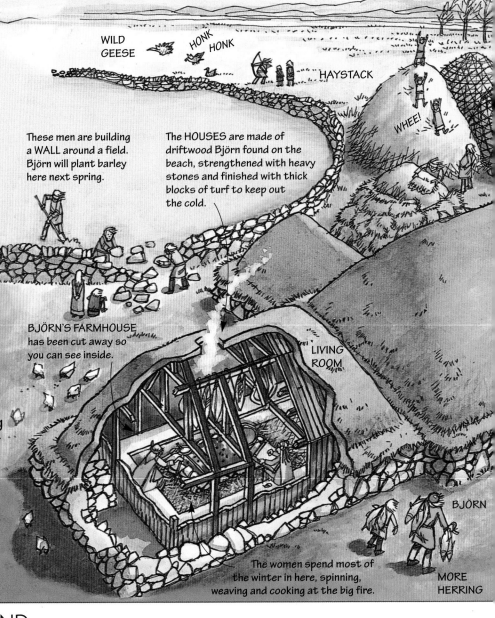

WILD GEESE

HONK HONK

HAYSTACK

WHEE!

These men are building a WALL around a field. Björn will plant barley here next spring.

The HOUSES are made of driftwood Björn found on the beach, strengthened with heavy stones and finished with thick blocks of turf to keep out the cold.

BJÖRN'S FARMHOUSE has been cut away so you can see inside.

LIVING ROOM

BJÖRN

The women spend most of the winter in here, spinning, weaving and cooking at the big fire.

MORE HERRING

SURVIVING IN ICELAND

SALTING MEAT

Edda needs lots of salt to preserve meat for the winter. She fills big cauldrons with seawater and salty seaweed, and boils them over a fire. When all the water boils away, salt crystals are left on the bottom.

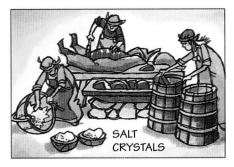

SALT CRYSTALS

Edda's friends help. One scrapes out the salt crystals, while another chops up a dead cow. Strips of the meat are packed in barrels with the salt. This helps stop the meat from going bad over the winter.

DRYING MEAT AND FISH

Edda dries out fish and chunks of meat, while a freeman shows his son how to light a fire of dried moss and twigs. He strikes a hard stone against some iron to make a spark and carefully lights the fire.

COLLECTING GRASS

These ANIMALS are being led in to shelter.

Whoa...

Everyone gathers to eat, work and chat in the HALL. There are low platforms along the walls for them to sit and sleep on.

ANIMAL BARN

PHEW!

REFUSE HEAP

EDDA

CLEANED FISH

Racks of COD and HERRING drying in the wind

NETTING BIRDS

In spring, thousands of guillemots and puffins make their nests on the cliffs. Although it's dangerous, settlers climb up the rocks to trap the birds. These men have caught lots to eat.

WHALING

Lots of whales live in the seas near Iceland. The settlers can eat whale meat, and melt down whale fat to use in oil lamps. Björn and his crew drive a small whale into shallow water and kill it with their spears.

HUNTING SEALS

Seals are also a useful source of food for the hungry settlers, and sealskins make good ropes and shoes. Two hunters creep up on some seals basking in the sun. They will spear the ones they can catch.

COLLECTING FEATHERS

NESTS

Eider ducks make their nests on the ground, and fill them with downy feathers to keep their eggs warm. These two women are collecting the feathers to stuff quilts and pillows. They also like to eat eider eggs.

A MEETING OF THE THING

Earl Knut and the other freemen from this area of Norway have come to attend a big meeting. This gathering happens a few times a year, and it is known as the Thing.

The men are here to discuss important local business matters, and to decide what to do with three criminals. Some of the freemen's wives have also come to join in the debate.

Everyone camps nearby, as the Thing will probably last for many days. It's a good opportunity for catching up on the gossip, doing a bit of trading, and joining in sports.

TRADERS

Viking punishments are often harsh. This woman is accused of being a WITCH. She will be stoned or drowned.

It was him!

OLEG

But I'm innocent!

This THIEF will have one of his hands cut off.

MAGNUS'S WIFE

KNUT

LAW SPEAKER

Knut and Astrid have a good reason to be here, as Oleg has been accused of murdering the blacksmith Magnus. Now everyone will decide if Oleg is guilty.

But Oleg is very stubborn, and refuses to answer any questions. One of the chieftains, who is chosen as law speaker, recites the Viking law to the crowd. They must all decide.

Everyone agrees Oleg is guilty. As punishment, he is banished from the land - he must leave Norway forever. He will have to go fast, as Magnus's family may try to kill him.

WEIGHT LIFTING

I win!

Vikings love to show off their great strength. These men are having a boulder-lifting competition to see who is the strongest.

WRESTLING

UGH!

Wrestling is also a popular sport. Each day after the talks are over, the freemen compete to see who is the best and strongest wrestler.

HORSE FIGHTING

OW!

Fierce, wild stallions are specially bred for fighting. Sometimes, during a horse-fight, the owners get so excited, they fight each other too.

WINTER FESTIVAL

Tonight, Knut and Astrid have invited all their friends to a festival at the farm. They hold one every winter. Astrid is well known for her good parties and delicious food.

The family is very excited. Feasts are always great fun, with poets and singers, dancing and drinking to entertain the guests. But there is lots to do before everyone arrives.

Erik has been out hunting for fresh deer and rabbits to be served at the feast. Astrid and Freyda prepare the food and drink. Sven collects wood for the fire. The children just play in the snow - it's much more fun!

WOOD FOR THE FIRE

SVEN

WHEEEE!

STORE HOUSE

ASTRID

KNUT

FREYDA

OOPH!

Slow down!

DRIED MEAT AND FISH

This SLAVE is clearing the snow off the ice. Some of the guests will come over the ice to get here.

Astrid has brewed this BEER specially.

DEER

ERIK

WOODEN SKIS

BONE SKATES

27

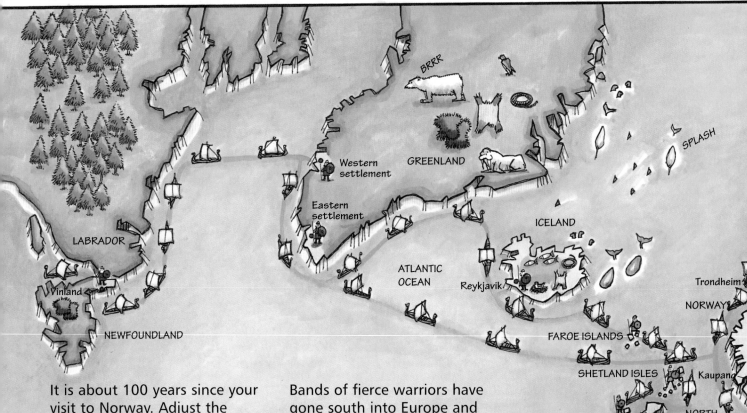

It is about 100 years since your visit to Norway. Adjust the destination readout on your time travel helmet, so you can hover above the places the Vikings explored and invaded since then. Vikings have raided all over Britain and Ireland, and settled down there to live, farm and trade.

Bands of fierce warriors have gone south into Europe and even as far as North Africa, to steal, kill and trade. In Central Asia they have traded with Arabs bringing silk from China. Many Norwegian Vikings have sailed west to explore and settle Iceland, Greenland and even the northern part of America.

WHAT THE VIKINGS FOUND

TIMBER	WEAPONS	JEWELS	POTTERY	FALCONS	ARABS
FURS	FEATHERS	WHEAT	GLASS	SPICES	SLAVS
WALRUS IVORY	SOAP-STONE	TIN	GOLD	SWORD BLADES	VIKINGS
HIDES	CLOTH	HONEY	AMBER	VIKING OVERLAND ROUTES	FRANKS
ROPES	SLAVES	SALT	SILVER	VIKING RIVER ROUTES	CARAVAN ROUTES
FISH	LOOT	WINE	SILK	VIKING SEA ROUTES	TRADING TOWNS

ARCTIC
OCEAN

Staraja
Ladoga

Bulgar

Novgorod

Birka

Grobin

Gnezdovo

SWEDEN

Wisikauten

Hedeby

Truso

Wolin

Kiev

R. DIEPNER

R. ELBE

Prague

SIGH!

ainz

Cracow

ITALY

R. DANUBE

Rome

Constantinople

TRAMPLE

R. VOLGA

ARAL
SEA

Tashkent

Samarkand

Bokhara

CASPIAN SEA

Gurgan

NATTER

BLACK SEA

R. TIGRIS

R. EUPHRATES

Baghdad

PERSIAN
GULF

CYPRUS

Sidon

Jerusalem

CRETE

Alexandria

TUG

SHOVE

MEDITERRANEAN SEA

NIBBLE

NORTH AFRICA

THE STORY OF THE VIKINGS

The first Viking raids began in about 793, when a band of Viking warriors attacked a monastery at Lindisfarne, a small island on the north-east coast of Britain. There the Vikings stole everything valuable in the monastery and murdered many people. News of this attack soon spread terror all over Europe.

A VIKING RAID

A year later, the raiders came back to England and attacked another monastery on the north-east coast. In the year 795, Vikings from Norway began raiding Ireland, killing and looting everywhere they went. About this time a few Norwegian Vikings settled on the Isle of Man (off England) and the Scottish islands.

VIKING SETTLERS

Other bands of Viking raiders sailed in their warships along the coasts of Germany, France Spain, Italy and North Africa. There they stole whatever riches they could find, killing and taking people as slaves.

RAIDERS WITH LOOT

Swedish Vikings went east to Russia, sailing down great rivers to raid and settle towns such as Staraja Lagoda, Novgorod on the Volchov river, Kiev on the Dniepner river and Bulgar on the Volga river.

SAILING THE GREAT RIVERS

At this time, the Vikings had their own gods, like Thor and Odin. Around 830, Ansgar, a monk, went to Birka to convert people to Christianity. But it didn't really work, and it was some time before most of the Vikings became Christians.

A MONK PREACHING

From the year 835, raids on England and Ireland became more and more frequent. Instead of making their usual quick hit-and-run raids, the Vikings set up camps and stayed on during the winter months. Then they began raiding again in the spring. Around 840 they settled in Ireland, building strong bases.

A WINTER CAMP

By now, many Vikings were leaving their homes to settle in other countries. Around 870 the first Viking farmers began to settle in Iceland. The Vikings had only discovered it about 10 years before. By 930 the whole island was covered with settlers. They set up their own parliament, the Althing.

THE ALTHING

Around 866, Danish raiders invaded England with a huge army and captured York. Soon Vikings were settled all over Northumbria. After 20 years of battles, King Alfred of England signed a treaty with the Danish leader Guthrum to divide up the country. The Danish part was called the Danelaw.

SIGNING THE TREATY

This treaty didn't bring peace. The Vikings continued to raid the English coasts and harass King Alfred. Around 926, when Athelstan was king, the English managed to recapture Northumbria from the Danes. But the Vikings were not completely defeated. They kept on attacking England for many years afterwards.

ATHELSTAN DEFEATS THE DANES

Early in the 10th century, bands of Vikings sailed from Ireland, attacking northwest England and overpowering the people who lived there. Many Vikings also settled in northern Scotland. In Ireland, Dublin and Limerick became important Viking trading ports.

VIKING DUBLIN

After almost a hundred years of attacks on mainland Europe, some Vikings settled there for good. In 911 Rollo, a Danish leader, captured a lot of land from the Franks in France. Their leader, Charles the Simple, gave Normandy to Rollo as Viking territory.

ROLLO AND CHARLES

Around 960, Harald Bluetooth, king of the Danish Vikings, decided to adopt the Christian religion for himself and his people. Three kings of Norway also tried for a long time to make their people become Christians. But many Norwegian Vikings continued to worship their own gods.

CHRISTIAN VIKINGS

Erik the Red, a Viking who had been banished to Iceland for killing a man, heard news of an unexplored island. Around 982, he sailed from Iceland to live on this land, which he called Greenland. A few years later he returned to Iceland, and persuaded many others to go and live in Greenland too.

ERIK THE RED IN GREENLAND

Around 1000, Erik's son, Leif Eriksson, sailed west from Greenland, and discovered an island which he called Vinland, after its grape vines. It was probably Newfoundland in America. Leif and some other Vikings lived there for a while.

LEIF SEES VINLAND

Late in the 10th century, more Viking attacks forced the English to pay money to keep their towns and people in peace. For several years the English gave the Vikings huge amounts of gold and silver, which was known as Danegeld. But the Vikings kept coming back for more, until 1016, when King Canute of Denmark invaded, and became king of England.

PAYING THE DANEGELD

Around this time, Christianity became the religion for all the Norwegian Vikings. They built churches and set up stones in memory of people who had died. These stones were carved with writing in runes (Viking letters), and were called rune stones. But some Swedish Vikings kept their own religion until the 12th century.

RUNE STONES AND A CHURCH

Christianity gradually changed the Vikings' way of life. They were not so fierce and no longer made so many raids or demanded Danegeld. By the end of the 11th century, the raids ended and the Vikings settled down to a quieter life. But they were still great traders all over Europe.

VIKING FARMERS

Wherever the Vikings settled they adopted the language and customs of the local people. They soon became French, English, Russian, Scots or Irish themselves.

Later, the people in Scandinavia, the Vikings' homeland, became known as Norwegians, Swedes and Danes. But even today in the countries where they settled, you can see the descendants of the tall, fair-haired and blue-eyed Vikings.

INDEX

This book was produced in consultation with Dr. D.M. Wilson
Usborne Publishing would like to thank the following for their help with this book:
Michele Busby, Philippa Wingate.
The time helmet illustrations on the cover and pages 1, 2 and 4 are by Toni Goffe.

First published in 1977 and revised 1997 and 2003 by Usborne Publishing Ltd,
83-85 Saffron Hill, London EC1N 8RT, England.
www.usborne.com
Copyright © 2003, 1997, 1993, 1990, 1977 Usborne Publishing Ltd.
The name Usborne and the devices ♀ ⊕ are Trade Marks of Usborne Publishing Ltd.
All rights reserved. No part of this publication may be reproduced, stored in a
retrieval system, or transmitted in any form or by any means, electronic,
mechanical, photocopying, recording or otherwise, without the prior permission of the publisher. U.E.
Printed in Belgium.
First edition published in the US in 1997.